Thomas B. McQuesten

Roland Barnsley

Fitzhenry & Whiteside Limited

Thomas B. McQuesten

Contents

© 1987 Fitzhenry & Whiteside Limited
195 Allstate Parkway, Markham, Ontario L3R 4T8

The Canadians: A Continuing series
General Editor: Robert Read
Editor: Frank English
Designer: McCalla Design Associates
Typesetting: Jay Tee Graphics Ltd.
Printed and bound in Canada

The Author
Roland Barnsley is a graduate of Queen's University and of
the Niagara Parks Commission School of Horticulture (1940).
In many ways, Roland is a protégé of T.B. McQuesten; he has
also contributed writings about McQuesten for a book
about illustrious Canadian Presbyterians, and to the television
program by John Best. He is a landscape consultant (OALA) in
St. Catharines, Ontario, and is a former superintendent of the
Niagara Parks Commission.

Canadian Cataloguing in Publication Data
Barnsley, Roland
  Thomas B. McQuesten

(The Canadians)
Bibliography: p.
Includes index.
ISBN 0-88902-894-X

1. McQuesten, Thomas B., 1882-1948. 2. Cabinet ministers —
Ontario — Biography.* 3. Civil service — Ontario —
Biography. 4. Ontario — Politics and government — 20th cen-
tury.* I. Title. II. Series.

FC3075.1.M37B37 1987   354.71304'092'4   C87-093919-X
F1058.M37B37 1987

Preface

Thomas Baker McQuesten (1882-1948) made
significant contributions to this country, especially
to the Province of Ontario. Some people make their
contributions in the arts, others in the sciences,
sports, education, management, or politics. The
latter two were T.B. McQuesten's primary routes to
achievement. He was an astute leader, manager,
and politician who skilfully used his intellect and
forceful personality to achieve his goals. Although
scrupulously honest, he was a shrewd bargainer and
acquired properties and materials at low or
reasonable prices to the advantage of the province.
His projects were accomplished openly and without
personal gain. A strong sense of modesty kept him
out of the public eye and, as a result, he is little
known. But in the building of great gardens and
parks, bridges and highways, McQuesten was a man
of enormous importance.

The most noteworthy of his works were all
completed in a mere decade, now 50 years past. All
have flourished and are now woven into the fabric of
Ontario's everyday life, its culture, and its future.
What the artist-builder created is with us today.
What is missing is his signature. This is the story of
these works and their "forgotten builder."

Chapter 1　A Memorable Day

The date was June 7, 1939. On this hot, humid, midsummerlike day, a most significant historic event held the attention of millions of Canadians, Americans, and in fact all of the English-speaking world. The first visit and tour of a reigning monarch and his queen to a British dominion was reaching a point of climax. Later that evening Their Majesties would board the royal train at Niagara Falls enroute to another first — four days in a foreign country, the United States of America! Much was to happen before that crossing of the Niagara River. Wednesday, June 7, proved to be the most taxing day of this demanding schedule. The King and Queen had appeared before hundreds of thousands of their loyal subjects in London, Ingersoll, Woodstock, Brantford, Hamilton, and St. Catharines before their arrival at Niagara.

Flags, banners, floral floats, and floral arches were everywhere. In many cities it seemed as if double the population had materialized, coming from all the neighbouring communities not included in the itinerary of the royal visit. All Canada took pride in putting forth its best for their King and

Reception for King George VI and Queen Elizabeth, June 7, 1939, at Administration Building, Niagara Parks Commission. T.B. McQuesten is at left of foreground group. Mackenzie King is at McQuesten's left, partly obscured.

Queen. Pride and patriotism abounded at every point. No one was more proud than His Majesty's loyal minister, the Honourable Thomas B. McQuesten, Minister of Highways for the Province of Ontario. As Chairman of the Niagara Parks Commission it was his duty to plan and act as host for the events to be held in Queen Victoria Park, at Table Rock on the edge of the awesome cataract, and at the signing of the impressive guest book at a brief reception in the Administration Building. Along with his pride, and compatible with his style, he no doubt relished the silent satisfaction of knowing that on that very day his king and queen had seen much of his greatest works. After all, they had spent the major part of the day in that immediate area so dear to his heart. From the moment when the gleaming, sleek, silver-and-blue train began to descend the great arch of the Niagara Escarpment into the Dundas Valley, and then crossed the expanse of the future Botanical Garden — later to be prefixed Royal — they were in his beloved country. Even from the train they would glimpse the noble pylons of Hamilton's High Level Bridge — an earlier monument to his determination to develop a majestic entrance to the city he loved.

Niagara Escarpment (background), Cootes Paradise, Princess Point (mid-ground), and Highway 403 in foreground, 1972

STEEL

High volume use of coal and iron ore by steel companies frequently placed Hamilton in the top three Canadian ports, based on tonnage handled annually.

Later they would skirt the city's other strength, perhaps not of aesthetic appeal, that of steel mills and the growing columns of blast furnaces. With the war clouds gathering over Europe, perhaps this element gave more assurance to the royal visitors than had the beauty of the land. Here, too, Tom could take pride, because his own grandfather had played a significant role in preparing the ground work for Canada's great steel industry. Like all stops that day, the one in Hamilton was as demanding as any, complete with a civic reception, a motorcade, and the applause of tens of thousands of children — all in Ontario's sticky summer heat.

Later in the afternoon a more refreshing hour would be enjoyed. The royal couple would leave the train, attend the St. Catharines reception, and then take the same beautiful drive sought by so many to this day. The Royal Cavalcade would wind through orchards and vineyards to Niagara-on-the-Lake and the remains of old Fort George. Thence they would proceed along the Niagara Parkway to Queenston and Brock's Monument and then on to Niagara Falls. The start of the motor tour gave Their Majesties a brief and effortless duty to perform.

Waterfront Hamilton Harbour & steel mills

Official Opening of Niagara Section of Queen Elizabeth Way, August 23, 1940. T.B. McQuesten is cutting the ribbon.

They rode in the lead car, a long, maroon Lincoln convertible with a chauffeur and a single aide in the front seat. Canada's first four-lane superhighway was dedicated by the very movement of their vehicle. At Niagara Street their route intersected a portion of the nearly completed throughway and, by the magic of the "electric-eye" beam, two Union Jacks dropped away to reveal the name of the new highway. The inscription read "The Queen Elizabeth Highway" named for Her Majesty and with her gracious consent. She and the King must have been pleased! Her husband would never live to see it equalled anywhere in the world. Nor would she, even in her much later years as the Queen Mother, see "Her Highway" surpassed.

In fact, in its time it was unequalled in America. Only the Autobahns of Germany were close in comparison. On completion to Niagara Falls, within a year, it provided a singular phenomenon. A motorist could drive its entire length to Toronto at night without the use of headlights. The few intersections or stoplights could be identified well in advance when the bright incandescent lighting changed to the amber glow of sodium-vapour lights.

An undertaking as vast cannot be credited to any

one man, but there cannot be any doubt that, as Minister of Highways from 1934 to 1943, Tom McQuesten provided his engineering staff with the incentive and dedication to build for the future and to build with excellence. After all, this was his hallmark and his legacy. Knowingly or not, Their Majesties would also encounter many other of his accomplishments on that busy afternoon of June 7, 1939. The Niagara Parks System was alive with development in the late thirties. In fact, the Niagara Parks System, founded in 1885 on the 62 hectares (154 acres) of Queen Victoria Park, only gained world renown following the great forward steps initiated by Chairman McQuesten. The entire west bank of the Niagara River from Fort Erie to Lake Ontario was developed and refined with ornamental horticulture to a standard never attained before in North America. Parks were his passion and joy!

One can only speculate as to how much the King and Queen were informed of the abilities and talents of this most impressive Minister of the Crown. Their actual time together, after lengthy formalities and introductions, was limited to a few moments or minutes at most. The Niagara Falls *Evening Review* reported the following day that the Chairman did have a brief audience with the Queen. The reporter who interviewed the Chairman immediately following, received glowing words and tributes to her beauty, her bearing, and her dress. When asked the nature of the conversation, the Chairman replied tersely that "he could not comment on that matter".

Hundreds of reporters and photographers attended the ceremonies. Newsreel films and still photographs were dispatched by the hundreds by the eager press for use in newspapers or theatres all over the world, but especially in Canada, Britain, and the United States. It is interesting that whoever shared centre stage with Their Majesties, it was never their host, the Chairman of the Niagara Parks Commission. Perhaps occasionally he was seen smiling in the background but never in the limelight. This modesty, too, was his hallmark.

There was much yet for him to do, but perhaps June 7, 1939, would be his fondest memory.

The McQuesten Family

Chapter 2

The McQuesten family had its roots in Argyleshire, Scotland. On the first step of a westward migration, they reached the Londonderry area in Northern Ireland. A generation later some members found it prudent, perhaps in the 1730s, to again look west to the new world and settled in New England. They established, amongst their numbers, homesites in various locations in the States of Maine, Vermont, and New Hampshire. They also acquired some wealth and developed successful careers. Perhaps most noteworthy to Canadians was Calvin McQuesten, M.D., the grandfather of Thomas Baker McQuesten. His life and career are well-documented in the archives of the family home, Whitehern, which is now maintained and preserved by the City of Hamilton.

Calvin McQuesten received the benefit of an extremely good education. He graduated from Bowdoin College in Maine with a medical degree. Fellow students at that time included such great American writers as Nathaniel Hawthorne, Henry W. Longfellow, and Daniel Webster. In addition to his scholarship and medical background, he exhibited at an early age great business skills and an understanding of financial affairs. Calvin succumbed to the family urge to move westward in search of greater opportunities and greener fields. He was not alone in this respect. The "Cultural Mosaic" of present-day Canada tends to mask the fact that the greatest contributer to the growth of Ontario's population was not Great Britain, nor France or Europe, but the New England states. Throughout the late 18th and 19th centuries and

Portrait of T.B. McQuesten's grandfather Dr. Calvin McQuesten

even later, Americans by the thousands arrived, following closely after the United Empire Loyalists, both "Early" and "Late". Western New York, Pennsylvania, Ohio, and Michigan received no preference over Ontario in this great western migration. It was not a matter of patriotism, but a sheer search for opportunity. These new settlers brought with them more than zeal; frequently they had funds, property, and, above all, skills well-suited for survival and prosperity in the "new west". Calvin was included in this group. In addition, he exhibited other great resources — caution and prudence. These qualities remained with him through the 50 years of his career that lay ahead.

His practice of medicine moved slowly westward from Maine to New Hampshire to Vermont and Western New York. Shortly after the development of the Erie Canal, Calvin established a practice in Brockport, New York (in the Rochester area). Before long he had acquired a pharmacy and some real estate holdings. He might have remained profitably in this happy location, but chance would dictate otherwise. A cousin, John Fisher, had moved one step further to the west and crossed the Niagara River to Upper Canada. In 1835, in a formal

Hamilton Ironworks—
McQuesten & Co.

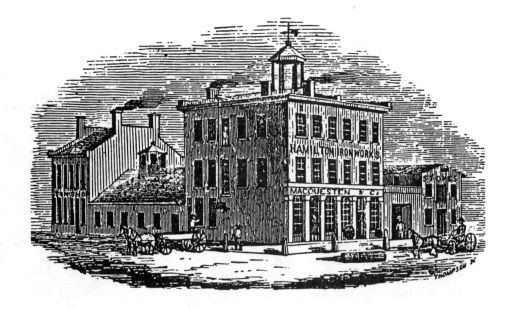

partnership, Calvin had joined with Fisher, Priam B. Hill (McQuesten's neighbour), and Joseph H. Janes of Upper Canada. It was their intention to duplicate the success of the well-known Backus firm of Brockport to which Hill had a close connection (his sister was married to a partner in the firm). The Backus firm had an excellent reputation in the design and development of high-quality and innovative farm equipment. From that date on Calvin commuted (not daily but frequently) by stage coach the distance between Brockport and Hamilton. The approximately 72 km (45 miles) from Hamilton to Niagara alone was frequently an 11-hour ordeal, in appalling conditions of mud and misery.

A McQuesten Stove at the William Lyon MacKenzie House, Bond St., Toronto

The early years of the foundry were equally difficult. Chronic shortages of supplies of pig iron, coal, and skilled workmen, as well as an unreliable transport system, presented painful problems to the businessman. Even greater difficulties plagued the colony which was still predominantly a bartering economy, woefully short of banks and currency. McQuesten's persistence paid off. Within ten years the company's success was assured. The firm successfully developed and patented Canada's first threshing machine. This was followed by a wide range of agricultural equipment, stoves, and other household objects for the expanding rural economy. By this time, transport had greatly improved, with the opening of a suitable channel through the Burlington Beach strip to give Hamilton a valuable harbour. Concurrently the Welland Canal, first completed in 1829, was beginning to realize its potential. As the firm prospered, a now wealthy John Fisher returned to New York State for other interests and to become a New York State representative in the Senate of the United States. Calvin McQuesten turned over the firm's operation to a nephew, Luther Sawyer. The demands of agriculture and the arrival of the railway era greatly increased the productivity of the firm. In its growth it becamse Sawyer-Massey, then Massey-Harris, and later Massey-Ferguson (now Varity), a name known worldwide in our generation.

Calvin's days of medical practice were behind him. His broad interests now ranged through the world of finance, with investments in banks, real estate, mortgages, and various business enterprises. He acquired a fine stone mansion, later known as Whitehern, in Hamilton. He is believed to have moved into the residence around 1847. It had been built on a grand scale, of limestone quarried from the face of the Hamilton mountain, by Richard Duggan, an attorney. Calvin purchased the house in 1852. It remained the McQuesten family home until the death of the last surviving member in the third Canadian generation, in 1968.

Dr. Calvin's first wife, Margaret Lerned died in 1841, having borne four children, three of whom died in infancy. The survivor, Calvin Brooks McQuesten, followed his father's medical career, but remained in the United States after taking his medical degree there. A second marriage, this to Ester Baldwin, produced another son, Isaac Baldwin McQuesten, who fathered the seven children of the final generation of McQuestens.

On arrival in Hamilton, Dr. Calvin McQuesten became immediately and deeply involved with the American Presbyterian Church, along with his cousins and their families. This involvement led to a deep and continuing commitment that extended with equal fervour and dedication throughout his family and all their descendants. His New England virtues continued to be fortified with the adoption of his new religion; he later embraced MacNab Street Presbyterian Church which was part of the Free Presbyterian Church of Canada.

The 1830s were years of great strife and agitation on the political scene. The Reform movement was seething with readiness for open rebellion. All American newcomers were perceived to be allies of the Reformers and a threat to the British way of life and government protected by the powerful Family Compact. The new American Presbyterian Church was particularly vulnerable, with some of its members in jail and its minister reluctant to face the coming storm. The church was forced to close. Dr. McQuesten was custodian of its assets, which he later turned over to the MacNab Street Church, which he and many of the old congregation had joined. In addition to this, it was

DR. CALVIN McQUESTEN AND SIR ALLAN MacNAB

Although contemporaries and both great contributors to Hamilton's growth, Dr. McQuesten and Sir Allan MacNab appeared to have had little communication. Their differences in politics, religion, and lifestyle were great. McQuesten, for all his investments, avoided railway stock and speculation but profited from the sale of his foundry production to the Great Western Railway promoted by MacNab.

reported that Dr. McQuesten also made a personal gift of $15 000 to the MacNab Street Church. His generosity was not restricted to finance. He served in a number of positions in the running of MacNab and the wider Church. Further, his and his family's presence were fully visible each and every Sunday, with the rarest of exceptions, for over 100 years — continuously! They were always in the pew second from the front.

His first son, Calvin Brooks McQuesten, was established by that time in medicine in New York State. The tone of family correspondence seemed to indicate that Calvin's father looked on him almost as a "defector". There is no indication that he shared in the old doctor's bounty or estate. Dr. Calvin had become at this point a fervent Canadian and a rabid supporter of his adopted city. During his lifetime, Hamilton had become Canada's third largest city and, in the view of its council, its most ambitious. In later years, a less reverent term, the "Lunch Pail Town", succeeded the more prestigious and favourable "Ambitious City". This, of course, was after the passing of the last McQuesten. Strangely, Dr. Calvin had contributed substantially to the justification of each name!

Calvin's attention now focussed on young Isaac Baldwin McQuesten, his heir apparent. His short career has been aptly summarized by the present incumbent of MacNab Street Presbyterian Church in Hamilton, the Rev. John A. Johnston, M.A., Th.M., Ph.D. His remarks follow: "Isaac, son of Dr. Calvin McQuesten, was educated at Dr. Tassie's school in Galt, at Upper Canada College, Toronto, and the University of Toronto. In 1865, this young 'red head', against his father's wishes, volunteered to serve in the 1st Service Company against the Fenians. A friend, disapproving of young McQuesten's action, wrote, 'It is calculated to throw you out in your whole course of study, before you are fairly started; and to you with the prospect of wealth, a finished education is the important thing.' After his premature discharge, Isaac completed his studies and was called to the bar, joining the law practice of William Proudfoot, later Chief Justice and Vice-Chancellor of the Supreme Court of

MacNab Street Presbyterian Church

Ruby Baker
1879-1911

Hilda-Bell
1877-1967

Muriel Fletcher
1880-1882

Rev. Calvin
1876-1968

Thomas Baker
1882-1948

Mary Baldwin
1874-1964

Isaac Baldwin 1847-1888
Married Mary Baker 1849-1934

Margaret Edna
1885-1935

First Wife
Margaret Lerned
1809-1841

Second Wife
Ester Baldwin
1816-1851

Third Wife
Elizabeth Fuller
? -1897
(no children)

(3 children died
in infancy)
Calvin Brooks
1837-1912

McQuesten Family Tree
Dr. Calvin McQuesten 1801-1885

Ontario. Proudfoot was a brother of the Professor of
Homiletics at Knox College, Toronto, as well as a
son of the first professor of the Secession theological
college in London, Ontario, who is recognized as the
father of the United Secession Church in Canada.

"For 16 years, Isaac McQuesten served on the
Board of Management of MacNab Street Church
and, in 1879, was elected to the Board of Education,
Hamilton. From 1881 to 1886, he acted on the
Senate of the University of Toronto, and was a
director of the Mutual Insurance Company of
Waterloo. He died prematurely in 1888 and, within
a decade, his vast empire, with investments in iron
at Madoc and Marmora, property in Hamilton,
together with various businesses, was assigned to
bankruptcy, with liabilities of almost a million
dollars."

*T.B. McQuesten's father,
Isaac McQuesten*

Isaac had married Mary Jane Baker in 1873. Her
father was to be the maternal grandfather of
Thomas Baker McQuesten and to some degree a
source of one of Tom's great interests, famous naval
vessels. Mary Jane's father had attained the rank of
Commander in the Royal Navy, with a distinguished
record in the sea battles of the Napoleonic Wars. In
1814 he was transferred to Upper Canada to serve
as Second-in-Charge on the "St. Lawrence" which
was one of the world's largest warships carrying
1000 men and 102 guns. Its formidable size and
armament were never challenged after it came into
service late in the War of 1812-14. Returning to
England, Commander Baker studied for the ministry
in the Congregational Church. By 1835 he had
returned to Kingston to erect the first
Congregational Church in Upper Canada. Later
ministries took him to Brantford and Newmarket.
On retirement he lived first in Toronto and
eventually in Hamilton with his daughter and son-
in-law and their growing family.

The first ten years of Isaac and Mary Jane's
marriage were very happy ones and produced seven
children, two sons and five daughters, one of whom,
Muriel the fourth daughter, died at the age of two.
The other six children thrived in generally good or
robust health; the first three children all attained
their nineties. Their first years of married life were

*T.B. McQuesten's brother,
the Reverend Calvin
McQuesten*

T.B. McQuesten's mother, Mary Baker McQuesten—as a young matron

spent in an attractive stone duplex scarcely more than 100 metres from the parental home. They also enjoyed the advantage of a summer residence in the Town of Hespeler, some 48 km (30 miles) away, where Isaac had extensive business interests.

The next five years were not so kind to Mary Jane. In 1885, old Dr. Calvin died at the age of 84, and in 1887, she lost her father in his 92nd year. Then suddenly, in 1888, she lost her husband, Isaac, who was only 41. His untimely death was a bitter blow, as it was coupled with the loss of virtually all the McQuesten fortune. Dr. Calvin, on retirement many years earlier, was said to be worth more than half a million dollars. Isaac's bankruptcy amounted to very near a million dollars. It was for the most part due to the failure of the Hespeler woollen mill that Isaac and his partner, John Harvey, so desperately had laboured to establish. In later years this same mill, under other owners (for many years Dominion Woollens & Worsteds Ltd.), would alternately bring grief and prosperity to the towns-people of Hespeler. The town fathers at one point

had invested town funds in the McQuesten
partnership (some $6000). Through World Wars I
and II the company had experienced tremendous
growth, so that the small town was dominated by
the mill's massive structure along the banks of the
Speed River. More than once, in alternate periods,
the doors were closed to business. This has been a
hard fact of life for the Canadian textile industry.

Mary Jane, at age 39, now faced a most difficult
life with six young children to rear and a great and
stately home to maintain with the most slender of
resources. For much of her remaining 46 years she
had to sustain and educate her family on an income
no greater than $1700 a year. Added to her grief,
were the circumstances of her husband's death. The
facts are now, and were then, unclear. The suspicion
of alcoholism and drug overdose clouds the exact
nature of his sudden death after a period of
despondency. Fortunately, her later years were
enjoyed in the success and attainments of her
youngest son in his legal and political career.
Thomas Baker McQuesten, both publicly and

*Mary Baker McQuesten and
family (left to right) —
Hilda, Thomas, Mrs.
McQuesten, Mary Jane,
Edna, Ruby, and Calvin*

privately, was never hesitant to shower his affection upon his mother and to give her full credit for his upbringing. More than once he referred to her as his "best chum".

She was indeed a remarkable woman. Her deeply religious background and her high moral convictions played an all-important roll in overcoming the difficult role that fate had delivered to her. Dr. Beverly Ketchen, the minister of her beloved MacNab Street Presbyterian Church (1905-46), knew her very well and provided this astute brief summary: "She had a real and puritanical sense of right and wrong . . . an uncompromising conscience . . . and inflexible integrity, kindliness, and graciousness." Others, less literate and perhaps less knowledgeable, have described her as being severe or, at the least, very stern. She contributed greatly of her time and of her meagre income to her church. Otherwise life was very limited, with the responsibilities of house and family and a minimum of social activity.

She played perhaps an inordinate role in directing the lives of her children, at least by the standards of today,if not in the norm of the last decade of the 19th century. It would seem that each had a prescribed role to play. Calvin, the oldest boy who had suffered a slight paralysis in one arm, was directed, although not inclined, to the ministry. The oldest two girls were retained to assist her in running the household. The third daughter, Ruby, pursued a gainful occupation as a teacher at the Ottawa Ladies College. Ruby was directed to provide financial assistance in the education of both Calvin and young Thomas. The youngest, Margaret Edna, appears to have been assigned no special role. Some health concerns may have contributed to this. She died at the relatively early age of 50, after spending a number of years in the Homewood Sanitarium at Guelph.

Tom had shown considerable promise at an early age in intellect and personality, and his mother looked for a great and successful career for him. She was not to be disappointed!

The Early Years

Chapter 3

Thomas was the sixth child and the youngest son of Isaac and Mary Jane McQuesten. He was born on June 30, 1882, in Hespeler (Cambridge, Ontario) at the family summer home. In those years, the family divided its time between the Bold Street residence in Hamilton and the Hespeler farm. His father had pursued his law practice with the prestigious and long-standing Hamilton firm, then known as Jones, McQuesten, and Chisholm. Thomas only briefly had the companionship of his father and two grandfathers. Little is now known of those relationships. Thomas is known to have sought, as a four year old, comfort from his mother after his father disciplined him for a minor act of disobedience. Later he would find a lot about his family from well-kept records and conversations concerning his ancestors, both recent and remote. He took great pride in his background and the well-known family virtues.

His schooling took place in the Hamilton school system where he attended Ryerson, Central, and Queen Victoria schools and graduated from Hamilton Collegiate with honours in English, History, and Classics. He was well-prepared for the university studies that followed. The days that followed opened up broad new worlds for Tom to conquer. Not only did he excel in academic studies at the University of Toronto, graduating in Honours in Political Science with gold medals in both Politics and Classics, but he took an active part in sports and social affairs, including the position of fraternity president. He held several posts with the Toronto *Varsity*, later becoming editor. He also found time to row with the Toronto Argonauts. In high school he had played football on the Hamilton Collegiate team which had won the Ontario Championship in 1900, and at a later date played with the Hamilton Tigers

*Thomas Baker McQuesten —
Age 5½ years*

At the University of Toronto — The Varsity *staff; T.B. McQuesten is centre, front row.*

ST. CLAIR BALFOUR

St. Clair Balfour was a prominent member of a Hamilton family well-known as wholesale food distributors and co-founders of Aylmer Foods. St. Clair's marriage into the Southam family was the start of the Balfour family's long association with the management of the Southam Press.

— the ancestors of today's Hamilton Tiger Cats. Squash, fencing, and golf all became part of his sports interests. Summers away from university brought him a vision of the much wider world.

During the summer vacation of 1901 he reached England and Scotland by working his way on a cattleboat, in his terms as "nursemaid to the bovine passengers". His travels in the land of his ancestors were extensive and may well have included the horticultural meccas and great public parks and gardens to which he later often made reference. He is reported as registering at the Canadian Pavilion in Glasgow in October of that year along with St. Clair Balfour — another Hamiltonian. His return voyage found him in the galley peeling potatoes for the whole crew, acquiring a deeply rooted and lifelong aversion to potato peeling. The two following summers found him in Quyon, Quebec, working as a lumberman, sorting logs on the swirling waters of the Ottawa River. He wrote to his brother Calvin begging him not to reveal to their mother the nature of his work for fear that she might have a fit. He undoubtedly achieved some skill at swimming during this vacation! After receiving his B.A. in 1904, he thought of applying for a Rhodes Scholarship. His credentials, academic and moral, and his likeable personality were all in his favour. He discussed the idea with his mother, accepted her advice, and withdrew. She had pointed out three obstacles to his possible selection. These were his family's religion, its political leanings, and above all the fact that he was from Hamilton and not Toronto! Instead, he entered Osgoode Hall to study law. There is no indication in the record that any other career had been discussed in the family or contemplated by Thomas. Certainly a career with his father's law firm would always be open to him.

He graduated from Osgoode, was called to the Bar in 1907, and articled for a short period of time in Toronto with Royce and Henderson. Before long, his roving spirit succumbed to the call of the North. The silver boom had arrived in Cobalt. Thomas headed north to a partnership in a law practice at Elk Lake in Timiskaming. Not far away, Arthur Slaght, K.C., was in practice in Haileybury. It is most likely that these two made their first contact in Ontario's north. Both were to play leading political roles in a future provincial Liberal Government. In 1909, however, he was impelled for family and personal reasons to return home to Hamilton and to enter his father's old firm as a junior.

It seemed that this would now be his career. The firm was at least as old as the city. Through a succession of partnerships, it had carried many famous names — Proudfoot, Craigie, Freeman, Munro, Jones, Chisholm, McQuesten, Logie, and now another McQuesten. The partners had a great deal in common, most were ardent Liberals and Scotsmen; many became judges later on; and most had a strong military connection. One (Logie) rose to the rank of Brigadier General and eventually became the commanding officer of M.D.2 headquartered in Toronto in the First World War. He also had been a founder of Hamilton's 91st Highland Regiment. Even Thomas had seen Militia Service during his university years, reaching the rank of Corporal with the Fourth Field Battery.

"Sartorial Perfection" — the young lawyer with his mother

On June 19, 1909 (June was always his favourite month), he began his career in the legal office with James Chisholm. This was to be his business home for the rest of his life, and intensively for the next quarter century. As a junior member, he was to receive very modest earnings for the next few years. In fact, in August of 1911, his mother felt that he should talk to Mr. Chisholm about the inadequacy. Ruby, his sister who had helped to support the family, passed away that year in the Gravenhurst Sanitarium from a common disease then called consumption, better known today as tuberculosis. However, in a few years Tom's career became firmly established, and his income and prospects continued to improve. His incisive mind, coupled with a sincere, if not warm, personality accumulated loyal clients to build a solid practice. In these early years he had ample time to develop a profound interest in the affairs of the day, especially in municipal affairs. His brother was away from home serving remote ministries in the North and the Canadian West. Tom's return to live again at Whitehern was a great source of comfort for his mother. Here he played a full role as the man of the house and in the day-to-day affairs of the household, in particular its financial support.

His first political step was taken in 1913, when he successfully ran as an aldermanic candidate. He maintained that position for seven successive years. These were dynamic years in the development of Hamilton and its immediate area. Its great strategic location, physically embraced by the shield of the escarpment, protected in climate, and endowed with the three great expanses of water ranging from Cootes Paradise on its west, the great harbour, Hamilton Bay, to the north, and the shores of Lake Ontario to the east all provided a setting unequalled in the vast expanse of inland North America. In the War of 1812-14, its military role was clearly understood. The great gravel ridge of Burlington Heights was the last bastion of defence against the invading Americans who had occupied the Niagara Peninsula and were in complete control of the Thames Valley. If it had fallen, the outcome of the war for Upper Canada could have had totally

different consequences. It was the daring offensive by the garrison under Colonel Harvey from these Heights that eliminated the American Army at Stoney Creek in the early morning hours of June 6, 1813.

One hundred years later, this same geography presented the city fathers with grave decisions in matters of city planning, zoning (in particular, railroad location), and, to those with foresight, the location of new roads and highways. It was in this arena that the young alderman developed skills and judgement that furthered his political career. He also learned that the best of plans could be fruitless if the political manoeuvres were not skilfully executed to the last detail. He was deeply concerned with one unrelenting problem. This was the location and re-location of rail lines. The very nature of Hamilton's site — a long and narrow shelf that lay on an east-west axis beneath the cliff face of the escarpment on the south, bordered by the Dundas Marsh (Cootes Paradise), The Bay, and The Lake to the north made for difficulty. The centre of the city was joined to the north by two constricted bars, the gravel deposit of Burlington Heights to the west and the sand spit of Burlington Beach in the east. It was paramount that the several convergent rail lines be limited in access and restricted to a prescribed section of the city, and served by one terminal rather than several.

It was in this era that many Canadian cities first became concerned with zoning and town planning. Authorities were few. The Engineering Institute of Canada only came into being in 1918. There were, however, some competent firms available, particularly on the subject of railway engineering. The Hamilton Council had engaged two of the very best, led by W.F. Tye and Noulan Cauchon. The latter, an accomplished railway engineer, was the son of Joseph Edward Cauchon, well-known in Quebec politics. A former mayor of Quebec, Joseph had once been asked to form the Government of Quebec in 1867. He had a seat in the federal government and was eventually to be appointed Lieutenant-Governor of Manitoba. These companies received the support of McQuesten and his committee for the adoption of their report, which called for the common terminal, appeared to have gained the approval of the Dominion Railway Board, but foundered in the Supreme Court on the issue of forcing the railways to adopt the proposal. Tom McQuesten learned a great deal from this campaign, as Cauchon's commission was extended to consider other planning matters, parks, highways, and beautification among them. It is ironic that Tom's beloved home, Whitehern, virtually, and later actually had the T.H. and B. (Toronto, Hamilton, and Buffalo) Railway in its backyard, almost from the time it was built, up to the present day. There would be many bitter struggles in the future with this unco-operative railway.

The family residence "Whitehern" — facing on Jackson Street, Hamilton

The International Railway Story

The first Commissioners of the Niagara Parks Commission
entered into an agreement with the Niagara Falls Park and River
Railway Company in 1881. In return for the provisions of right-of-
way to operate a scenic railway through the Park's prime lands,
the Commission would receive fixed revenues each year
amounting to $10 000 per year for 40 years. It also included a
renewal agreement: if not exercised the company was to be "duly
compensated" for their railway and other assets. In *1932* the
company, now virtually bankrupt with declining revenues and
horrendous problems in maintaining its right-of-way, ceased
operation and sought compensation from the N.P.C. The (now)
International Railway Company was awarded $179 000 by
arbitration. An appeal on their behalf in the Supreme Court of
Ontario reduced the amount to $169 000.

The company again appealed to the highest level — The
Privy Council in the United Kingdom in *1937* — and was
awarded an enormous sum in excess of $1 000 000. Because of
subsequent litigation over interest, the Commission was ordered
to pay more than $1 500 000 in *1942*. It seems that the British
justices were unaware that the assets of the company were now
largely rust, or perhaps they were standing on an archaic
interpretation of "duly compensated", or, as some have suggested,
British authorities have historically deferred to the Americans in
Canadian-U.S. disputes — particularly in times of stress. At any
rate, this case highlighted the need for Canada to end the
constitutional need to seek ultimate justice in the "Mother
Country". The millstone of this debt restricted development for
another 14 years.

Oddly enough, an act of God, early in 1938 provided an ironic
twist of revenge. The Upper Arch Bridge, owned by the
International Bridge Company, was moved from its abutments by
an unusual pile-up of ice in the river below. This effectively ended
their rights to a bridge at this location. The door was opened for
McQuesten to plan immediately for the new Rainbow Bridge to
complement the new Oakes Garden Theatre. Strikingly beautiful
and complete with a Carillon Tower, it replaced one of the
remaining eyesores in the immediate area of the Falls.

There were other defeats. Tom had supported the cause of public gas distribution but had to yield the service to private enterprise. Nevertheless, he had acquired a broad base of understanding in the matter of planning and building for the greater good and also of the uncertainties that could arise in the political process. He was well-prepared for the public service career that lay immediately ahead.

By 1922 he reasoned that there would be much greater scope for his talents and for positive results if he selected another arena. He chose the Hamilton Board of Parks Management. It was a wise choice! His appointment to the board was made by council on the death of a member in July 1922. Provincial legislation had been enacted through the Public Parks Act—Ontario to create autonomous boards. In essence, a Parks Board could demand from City or Town Council a certain percentage of the municipality's tax revenue (to certain limits) for operational purposes and also capital funds, to a less restricted limit. The city fathers could scream but, in the final showdown, they were required to provide the funds. If this sounds like the present-day Boards of Education — it is! Their powers were exactly the same. Only one now remains, and it is not the Board of Parks Management.

Tom McQuesten had now reached a kind of heaven. Within ten years, Hamilton would have the largest acreage of developed parkland in any Canadian city. Not only the largest, but it would include the most scenic, the best-planned and executed, and the best variety in form and theme. It must be made clear that this growth could not be attributed totally to T.B. He was one part of a "dynamic duo". The other member was C.V. Langs, Q.C.

C.V. Langs was Chairman of the Board and new member McQuesten became Chairman of the Works Committee. They had much in common: both were lawyers skilled in the transactions and values of real estate. They were very development-minded and very ambitious for the "ambitious city". They worked so well as a team that each remained in office for over 20 years—working together! They enjoyed every minute. They acquired lands by every

legal means, much of it far beyond the city's then built-up area. Some was acquired parcel by parcel, by purchase, by gift, by tax arrears, and by barter and exchange (gaining land area on every exchange). It would be impossible to credit one more than the other — they were simply a terrific team. It is likely that McQuesten played a leading role in development. From a great affection for fine gardens, partly acquired in the family gardens at Whitehern and partly from his travels to Britain, he demonstrated a deep knowledge of garden possibilities and their needs. Also to be considered was a unique ability to recognize and utilize only the best of talent in a consulting or advisory role. Landscape architects were a rare breed in the 1920s. Most were imports. Nevertheless, T.B. found and used the best of them and frequently! For an unknown profession, Hamilton had become a Mecca. Quibbling on the costs of plans, plant materials, and replacements was the norm of the day. Most often, payment was deferred by the Board and was later settled by the Works Committee Chairman in a suitable compromise, with an advantage usually to the client.

Gage Park — an early aerial view of the large neighbourhood park situated in the "Delta District" at the foot of the mountain. The formal, informal, and recreational areas are clearly discernible, along with the greenhouse ranges. Along with these amenities, the area residents enjoyed the fragrance of orange blossoms each winter. The aroma, however, did not come from the park! It was a by-product of the Wagstaffe Jam & Marmalade Company adjoining the park on its western boundary.

The list of parks that were created is lengthy. One of the first milestones was Gage Park. When the first land was purchased, it was done with Alderman McQuesten's support of the proposal that had been made by one John E. Brown in 1913. The Gage Farm was outside the City at that time and the idea seemed far-fetched to the Council. Years after Brown had died, McQuesten at last bought the property for the Parks Board. H.B. Dunington-Grubb was selected as designer and employed a blend of formal and informal themes for this large attractive area in Hamilton's then East End.

The grand official opening is best described by a quotation from Marjorie Freeman Campbell's book *A Mountain and a City*. Governor General Viscount Willingdon was in attendance.

"The day had been carefully planned. A platform held the vice-regal couple, civic officials, and local notables. To the south of the fountain, in a roped enclosure, sat several hundred guests admitted by ticket. About this static core on the well-groomed lawns and among the bright flower beds, the public crowded.

"Following earlier events, C.V. Langs, Parks Board Chairman was to speak briefly, concluding with a request that Lady Willingdon receive flowers to be presented by young Jane Treleaven, the mayor's daughter. His Excellency would then declare the fountain unveiled, and simultaneously T.B. McQuesten would casually raise his handkerchief, at which signal an alerted attendant would turn on the fountain.

"Unfortunately, well before Lord Willingdon's programme participation, a guest on the platform took out his handkerchief and to general astonishment the fountain sprang into full play, just at a moment when the summer breeze gusted from the north, thoroughly spraying guests in the enclosure, before the water could be shut off.

"When the programme resumed, Mr. Langs announced the presentation of flowers and Lady Willingdon graciously indicated her acceptance. An embarassing pause ensued. There were no flowers. Laughing heartily, Lady Willingdon asked that Jane be presented to her. Later, at tea in the clubhouse, the errant bouquet arrived."

Other parks followed rapidly in succession. Every scenic opportunity was taken, every neighbourhood received consideration, whether for recreational use or beautification or land preservation. Before this time, the city had a playground system. This too was improved and expanded with organized programmes and supervision. Council sometimes winced at the expenditures but took considerable pride in the results. In retrospect, there is no doubt that funds were well spent and added immeasurably to the city's prestige and quality of life. In fact, the Board's contribution to the city was much more tangible. This can be seen from the following examples which deserve particular mention.

Langs and McQuesten acquired several large parcels of land at the western end of Hamilton on a rich plateau overlooking Cootes Paradise (the Dundas Marsh). It was their policy to acquire lands for park purposes in advance of need, for greater economy and better planning. It was a beautiful blend of productive open land, forest slopes, and marshlands. There is evidence that the botanical garden concept was already taking form, certainly in the minds of this pair of leaders. The site was suited admirably for the purpose and celebrated for its panoramic view of the entire valley, escarpment, and city. In the same decade (1920s), McMaster University in Toronto had reached a decision to replace its outmoded facilities and seek a new location.

At that time, Ontario could claim only two university centres (Toronto and Kingston) of status. A fledgling university had been started in London and a few small colleges were in existence in other Ontario cities and towns. Competition to secure McMaster was intense. The offer by the City of Hamilton to provide, at no cost, the magnificent Westdale site tipped the scales in its favour. The Baptist Trustees of McMaster were impressed but not totally convinced. Two events finally clinched the decision, a local fund-raising drive, the "Bring McMaster to Hamilton Campaign", and the offer by the prestigious Board of Parks Management to provide magnificent landscaped grounds. The first Chancellor at McMaster, H.P. Whidden, in later years frequently testified to the role of McQuesten in the trustees' decision. The University and the City bonded, to the great benefit of both.

The Parks Board lived up to its promise! The campus was reached by a long approach road from Main Street. Immediately on completion, the once open field held a broad avenue tastefully bordered with white birch and a harmonious selection of dark green conifers. At its mid-point near King Street was set a long, classical sunken garden with a

A 1950 picture of the Great American Elm on the McMaster campus.

The Lily Pool at Sunken Gardens of McMaster University, 1950

formal pond to attract all visitors with its wealth and variety of plant material. To the west stood the great "Patriarch" of all American elms. This massive tree rose a clear 18 m (60 feet) before branching. Its head stood over 30 m (100 feet) from the ground and was virtually as wide. Both the elm and the sunken garden have disappeared: one to disease and old age, the other to the burgeoning growth of an expanding campus. This project was carried out by Dunington-Grubb and the materials of his Sheridan Nurseries.

On a totally different subject, the Board of Parks Management at almost the same time gave the city another great distinction. Hamilton was to become the birthplace of the British Empire Games (now known as the British Commonwealth Games). The city had held a significant position in the world of sports. In football, the exploits of the Tigers antedate the McQuesten-Langs era by more than two generations, and the city was to be rewarded later with the Canadian Football Hall of Fame. It sits majestically next door to the McQuesten family home. This surely must be sheer coincidence! In the twenties, the city had provided a great impetus to sports, in particular to track-and-field and rowing. This perhaps could be traced to the great champions of earlier days, Bobby Kerr in the Olympic Marathon of 1908 and his contemporary, the great Tom Longboat. When the promoters sought to create a second Olympics by holding an all British Empire

BRITISH EMPIRE GAMES. HAMILTON. ONT. AUG 16-23. 1930

Closing ceremonies of the First British Empire Games (later Commonwealth Games) at Hamilton. Inset are the flags of the 11 competing countries. On the Maple Leaf dais is renowned Canadian Sprinter Percy Williams of Vancouver, flanked by the representatives of Hamilton's two celebrated regiments — the 91st Argyll & Sutherland Highlanders and the Royal Hamilton Light Infantry. Eleven of the distinguished competing athletes are also included.

1. *Percy Williams — Canada — World's Champion Sprinter and Olympic Champion 1928*
2. *H.B. Hart — South Africa — Discus and Shot-Put Champion*
3. *Greg Power — Newfoundland — Champion Sprinter and Jumper*
4. *O.Mc.L. Wright — Scotland — Marathon Winner*
5. *Miss V. Davies — Wales — Swimming Champion*
6. *Lord David Burghley — England — Hurdler Champion*
   (aiso Olympic Champion in 1928 in 100-m hurdle)
7. *W.J. Saridan — New Zealand — Winning Miler*
8. *Don Sendbuck — Bermuda — Swimming Champion*
9. *A.T. Matres — British Guiana — Oarsman*
10. *W. Britton — Northern Ireland — Champion Hammer Thrower*
11. *H.W. "Bobby" Pearce — Australia — British Empire and Olympic Champion — Single Sculls*

Games in the years between Olympic Competitions, they approached the Board of Parks Management for support. Sensing the opportunity, McQuesten and Langs immediately began planning. As it has been ever since, the need for facilities was the immediate target. A park, a stadium, and a pool would be the minimum! The investment would be enormous. Numerous committee meetings were held; budgets were proposed and slashed. That is, until McQuesten, tired of debate and a skimpy approach, made it clear that he would not countenance that attitude. It was "either do the job right, or don't do it at all." With the air cleared, the project moved ahead quickly. The swimming pool was built, complete with a roof and gallery (the roof had been considered expendable by one of the frugal committee members). The great concrete stadium, complete with press box, arose in the field that was once Scott Park. The institution that became the British Commonwealth Games was now underway. The completed facilities became a solid contribution to the City's sports life and stand to the present day. The seating and the names have changed, as have the participants. Scott Stadium eventually became the home field for the Hamilton Tiger Cat football

The original presentation plan by the award-winning firm Wilson, Bunnell & Borgstrom. The proposal embraced an area of over 6.5 km², from Eastwood Park on the left to Cootes Paradise and the lands of the Royal Botanical Gardens on the right. The detailed draftsmanship was the work of K.M. Broman. Many of the detailed features were incorporated into the immediate development. A notable exception is the waterfront boulevard extending from Wellington Street to Woodland Cemetery and the present headquarters area of the Royal Botanical Gardens.

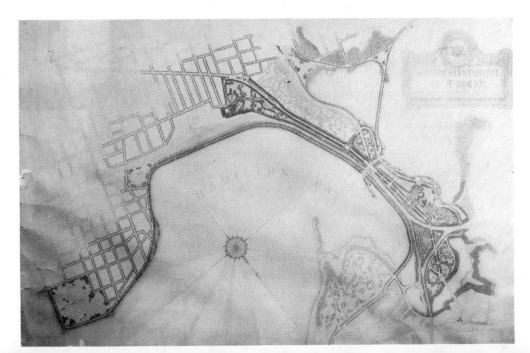

team. It is no longer Canada's largest stadium but a great place for the spectator — no binoculars are needed to find the players.

In reading the city page of either the Hamilton *Herald* or *Spectator*, a visitor would note that, column for column, the affairs of the Board of Parks Management outnumbered all other city activities by at least two to one. A steady stream of development and beautification plans was conceived, adopted, and developed, within the span of the late twenties.

The project that had lain dormant since McQuesten's early aldermanic years was again advanced. This was the North West Entrance Master Plan. It involved, as earlier suggested by Cauchon, a comprehensive treatment for railways, highways, and bridges to direct traffic into Hamilton from the north and west. The focus of the plan was the gravel ridge of Burlington Heights extending north and west from the grounds of Dundurn Castle for nearly two kilometres to headlands of the north shore. At that time the Heights were an unsightly array of shanties, gas stations, and gravel pits which threatened the existence of the entire ridge. Action had now become a priority. On McQuesten's suggestion, it was decided to offer a prize for the best proposal for the development of this critical area and its adjacent lands. Perhaps the greatest example of his political skills, based on his intelligence and integrity, is the fact that the North West Entrance Development gained the total

The New High Level Bridge on completion. Note the crested pylons and the empty niches. Over 55 years have passed since the proposal to put statues of famous Hamiltonians in these cavities was advanced by McQuesten. The City of Hamilton in 1987 formally named the bridge "The Thomas B. McQuesten High Level Bridge".

support of a Labour régime in City Council, and a Conservative Government in Ontario. It was quite an accomplishment for an avowed *Liberal*.

Many entries were received from leading architectural, engineering, and landscape practitioners. The award was given in 1928 to the Toronto firm of Wilson, Bunnell & Borgstrom. The presentation drawing was prepared with infinite care and expressive detail by a young Swedish landscape architect, K.M. (Matt) Broman. Its scope was enormous. It reached from the present Royal Botanical Gardens Headquarters, past the grounds of Dundurn Castle, to the Harbour front at Wellington Street. The future Rock Garden and a host of other features, from small hidden gardens, raised lookout points, boulevards, and avenues of trees to waterfront developments, all were detailed meticulously. It was truly a master plan! So attractive was its concept that implementation was almost immediate and most of the principal elements were completed within a few short years.

The City Engineer played a leading role in fulfilling the Plan with the creations of civil engineering. That man was W.L. McFaul and the new High Level Bridge became his monument. McQuesten was the first to give credit to McFaul for building this massive, but beautiful structure. McFaul expressed his gratitude by giving full gredit to McQuesten for providing the opportunity. The grandeur of the bridge can be credited to the enormous tapered pylons erected at each of its four corners. Their function was strictly decorative, performing no structural role. Each pylon was provided with a niche facing the roadway. These spaces were large enough to hold a greater-than-life-size statue. The statues were never installed!

Perhaps the reason is given best by Paul Wilson, in a recent issue of the *Spectator* and quoted here as follows:

WHY FOUR HAMILTON VIPs HAVE NO NICHE

Thirty-five thousand cars zip over the old High Level Bridge on York Boulevard every day.

If you stood out there and stopped all those drivers, you wouldn't find one who could tell you the tale of the missing statues.

Here it is — unburied at last, after more than 50 years of stony silence.

And now is a good time to go public with the facts, because $2.4 million is about to be pumped into the decaying span.

It was 1931, the year construction on the bridge began — part of a spectacular new entrance to Hamilton, along with the development nearby of the Royal Botanical Gardens' Rock Garden.

The bridge design was the result of an international competition, and included four three-storey-high pylons. Built into each of these was a cavity — some people call it a niche — big enough for a statue, complete with a built-in pedestal.

That's where our deep-throat — 78-year-old, not-yet-retired lawyer Adam C. Zimmerman — comes into the story.

According to him, Thomas McQuesten, a Hamilton Liberal who was the province's Minister of Highways at the time, sent letters to the families of four prominent city men: the late Adam Zimmerman, an MP and grandfather to our informant; the late Sir John M. Gibson, former Lieutenant-Governor of Ontario; the late Colonel William Hendrie, soldier and businessman; and Major-General S.C. Mewburn, Canada's minister of defence during the First World War.

The proposal to each family was simple: If they got bronze likenesses made of the hero in their family, the province would place the statues in the pylons when the bridge opened.

"I remember the talk among our family," says lawyer Zimmerman. "We were all pretty excited. We wondered who'd do it and how much it would cost. But I remember it was decided dollars were not going to be an obstacle, even if we went bankrupt."

Family Compact
But then came the charges of "family compact" — the four men to be honoured all represented the influential Presbyterian church.

"The cries rolled in from the Anglicans, the Methodists, the Baptists," said Mr. Zimmerman. "Then the whole idea collapsed. And those pylons have been empty to this day."

There's no mention of the quarrel in the Hamilton *Spectator* files of the early thirties. But nearly 20 years later the city's controller pushed a plan to turn the High Level Bridge into a monument for Hamilton's leaders.

"The cost of the statues could be raised by public subscription," said Walter Chadwick in the summer of 1949. He made no reference to the original Famous Four.

He felt Nora-Frances Henderson — a journalist and stormy debater who became Hamilton's first woman on city council — should be first to be honoured.

"Each statue could have a tablet with it," said the controller, with details of the person's work. "This is a spot that is passed by thousands of visitors and citizens daily. It is an ideal location for such a memorial."

Perhaps, but the idea of putting Miss Henderson on the bridge never surfaced again.

There was one more attempt to turn the bridge into a memorial. On Jan. 4, 1952, *The Spectator* carried a picture of a pylon, with an arrow pointing to the niche. The caption underneath read:

"Bridge of Memory? A proposal that a bust or plaque in memory of the late Hon. T.B. McQuesten be erected in one of the niches of the High Level Bridge will be made at the annual meeting of the Hamilton Horticultural Society this evening. Mr. McQuesten was the inspirer of the city's west entrance, with its gardens and boulevards. In the same proposal will be a clause suggesting the renaming of the bridge 'McQuesten Bridge'."

There's not another word on what happened to that idea.

Hamilton has now applied to designate the bridge under the Ontario Heritage Act. Once that's done, the province will kick in up to $150 000 for the $2.4-million renovation job.

Next year, the road deck will be torn up, the steel trusswork and ornate railings sandblasted and painted and old lamps that have been gone for decades replaced. Bike paths may be worked into the bridge's wide sidewalks.

There's no word yet on the celebrations for the rebirth of the High Level Bridge. But Adam C. Zimmerman thinks it might finally be time to find four tenants for these empty niches. And he's not suggesting his grandfather.

Since publication of this article, the bridge has been renamed the McQuesten High Level Bridge!

For the actual construction of the park and garden of the Northwest Entrance, McQuesten needed the most able landscape supervisor he could obtain. He chose well. He secured Matt Broman who had led the Borgstrom team to success in securing the design assignment.

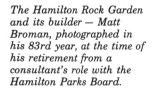

The Hamilton Rock Garden and its builder — Matt Broman, photographed in his 83rd year, at the time of his retirement from a consultant's role with the Hamilton Parks Board.

In these years, the paralysis and frustration of the Western world's greatest depression had arrived. Development had stagnated and unemployment had reached levels never equalled before or since. This did not deter McQuesten. Using "relief" labour provided by the city on a three-day cycle, the great Rock Garden was constructed. When completed, it brought international acclaim to the city. It became the first significant unit in the old dream of developing in Canada a major botanical garden. Initially it was a function of the Board of Parks Management.

The rock garden was created by the transformation of a deep gravel pit, using thousands of tons of weathered limestone rocks gathered and trucked from the escarpment face of Hamilton. All were placed most carefully under the watchful eyes of the new superintendent, Matt Broman.

The successful launching of the North West Entrance Project did not prevent the planning and development of a galaxy of other parklands. Included were the acquisition of Albion Falls and adjacent lands to provide the great natural park of Kings Forest, the development of Hamilton Mountain face lands, the acquisition of the Chedoke Golf Course, and that of the old radial car right-of-way to Ancaster. In all, long fingers of green parkland reaching to the city's core were claimed for the future. These still exist. This panorama is not seen by today's motorist speeding over the Burlington Skyway. However, from the mountain face and its lookout points, the city below still stretches under a green mantle to the harbourfront with its massive concentration of heavy industry.

ROCK GARDEN

Contrary to popular belief,the rehabilitation of gravel pits and quarries is far from a new concept. Three of Canada's best-known gardens have used this method. Montreal's Botanic Garden and the Hamilton Rock Garden date back over 50 years. The Butchart Gardens of Victoria are closer to a century old. Another great quarry garden may be built in the near future. The Province of Ontario has recently acquired a large site adjacent to Queenston Heights Park, the original Queenston Quarries which operated for some 150 years. This was the source of so much of the McQuesten stonework seen in the Niagara Parks System. The Niagara Parks Commission will have custody of this 40-ha site.

Chapter 4 The Larger Arena

It was inevitable, as a serving alderman, that T.B. McQuesten, with a passionate interest in development, beautification, town planning and zoning, and his desire to create in Canada the ideal environment, would look to the greater sphere of provincial politics. The ultimate decisions could only be legislated in the realm of provincial government. Here his talents could be fully realized. His initial attempt to obtain a seat was made in 1923. He was not successful. The Conservative Party won the day. Tom would have to bide his time! This was not difficult. His numerous interests with the Board of Parks Management represented a virtual full-time occupation. His law practice flourished in the general good spirits of the twenties. He was able to improve noticeably the quality of life for his mother and dependent sisters. Personally he enjoyed the extensive family garden, his walks with associates and friends in Hamilton's downtown, and time spent at the Brookdale Trout Club. He was extremely personable, above average height with a rugged physique and athletic build. His grooming and clothing usually brought admiring comments from women. Many fashionable ladies were quite prepared to drop other interests if they chanced to encounter Thomas on a stroll. His male friends were equally impressed, and friendships once made were long standing. His intimates preferred to call him "Tim".

Family correspondence shows great affection, not only for his mother but also for his sisters and his brother, Calvin. The latter in his wanderings showed little interest in finance. Tom frequently sent reminders from his law office that payments on obligations were either pending, due, or perhaps even overdue. In one instance, Calvin apparently made an unfortunate property sale. Offering sympathy and advice, T.B. described the purchaser as "a thoroughly disreputable and unscrupulous scoundrel" but he would do what he could to assist Calvin in collecting the money.

In the summer of 1924 Thomas found time to sail once again across the Atlantic to Britain. No need to peel potatoes or tend cattle this time! This trip was undertaken in a style befitting his status as an established solicitor and man of affairs. The reason for the trip was the invitation of the British Bar Association to their Canadian and American counterparts to attend its annual meeting and convention in England. In addition to their serious deliberations, there were elaborate tours, parties, and social gatherings. The delegates were shown every courtesy throughout the realm. They were fêted at numerous country homes and historic sites, and were introduced to royalty and to Britain's leaders. Tom's mother, Mary Jane McQuesten, was able to accompany her son. Perhaps this was the highlight of her declining years. Her son undoubtedly included visits to the great Botanic Gardens at Kew and Edinburgh in the itinerary!

That year, 1924, was also momentous for the Presbyterian Church. For more than 10 years, discussion and debate had taken place over the matter of Church Union involving several Protestant denominations (Methodist, Presbyterian, and Congregational). Initially, the members of the MacNab Street church appeared to show some preference for union. As the debate carried on, the momentum swung to the opposite position. Tom and brother Calvin took opposite views, each vehement in his attitude — so much so that they were reported to have engaged in a shouting match at a congregational meeting on the subject. When the final vote was held in December 1924, Calvin found himself in a somewhat untenable position — the lone dissenter in a family of six that favoured the "Continuing Presbyterian" position!

On the political front, Tom continued his activity with the Liberal Party. The party was now approaching nearly 30 years of barren political exile in Ontario, particularly in Hamilton. His loyalty was acknowledged. He was awarded the vice-presidency of the Ontario Liberal Association in 1931, and two years later he became its president.

As life frequently shows, he proved to be the right man in the right place at the right time. The winds of change were in the air. In 1933 the full impact of the Great Depression had clamped a great vise on the economy of Canada and the world. Voters in all democracies were ready to vote for a change as an alternative to the frustrations of unemployment and its grave social consequences. However, Canadians would need some assurance as to the quality and substance of the party offering an alternative to the existing Conservative Government.

There were two prime needs for success. One was the selection of a leader who would be dynamic, credible, and an orator. The political speech was still the great criterion for political success, both in the public meeting and increasingly so in the new medium of radio, which now was found in nearly every home. The other need was a strategy. It did not take McQuesten and his fellow members too long to arrive at solutions for each. The provincial party had to reach out to the federal field to find the leader with the qualifications they needed. There they found the member for West Elgin — a backbencher in Mackenzie King's government since 1926. The selection may not have pleased all

Prime Minister William Lyon Mackenzie King signing an agreement in his office on Parliament Hill, Ottawa, in the late 1930s.

provincial Liberals, but certainly on results the party had chosen the right man — Mitchell Hepburn.

The party executive, under McQuesten, adopted a strategy of humiliation and derision of the Conservative incumbents. Their new leader had little difficulty in portraying the Conservative leaders as inept, laughable, and incompetent. "Mitch" was quick-witted and completely in tune with the "common man". Success was assured.

Neil McKenty, in his book *Mitch Hepburn* (McClelland & Steward, 1967), made the following summation: "When all the factors in the 1934 political upheaval, including the dimension of the sweep, are examined, one factor stands out: the leadership of Mitchell Hepburn. For the first time in 30 years the Liberals offered a genuine alternative to the ruling régime (George Henry and the Conservatives) at Queen's Park. That alternative was not so much a programme as a man." The definitive study of that political era in Ontario has not yet been completed, but most analysts uniformly give the Hepburn Government full marks for efficiency and good government. A substantial part of that good government was Thomas Baker McQuesten.

On July 10, 1934, McQuesten was sworn in by the Lieutenant-Governor as a cabinet minister with two portfolios, Minister of Public Works and Minister of Highways. Not long after, he was appointed Chairman of the Niagara Parks Commission. He also maintained his position on the Hamilton Board of Parks Management.

No new minister came better prepared for his assigned duties than Tom McQuesten. His 20 years of apprenticeship with roads, bridges, and town planning would serve him well. His university career, legal experience, and real estate knowledge meshed perfectly with his new positions. He also knew that his ministry would be well-funded. The widespread use of the automobile was adding ever-increasing revenues through gasoline tax and vehicle licences. Outside the Treasury headed by the Premier, the Highway Ministry was the province's largest revenue producer. By double good fortune, The Niagara Parks Commission, a Crown agency of

The Lion at foot of column, Queen Elizabeth Way, at the Humber River, Toronto.

the province, was also self-funding, with the potential for much greater growth. There was no need to make small plans. He could build for the future and build on a grand scale. He proceeded with vigour and with vision in both of his new offices.

Attendant to the change of government, came the sweep of the "new broom". There was much advance speculation as to the extent of change and its direction. Great benefits to Southwestern Ontario, probably at the expense of "Hogtown" (Toronto), were prophesied. Certainly, some degree of new staff appeared in the usual places for patronage, particularly among the minor officials of the liquor "dispensaries" and also among the licensees of "beverage" rooms. These matters were of little or no concern to the new Minister of Highways. In his years of effort in creating the "North West Entrance" he had learned to appreciate the talent of the Highways Department, with whose members he had frequent consultations. The senior management included the two Smiths — not brothers. They were R.M. Smith as deputy minister and A.A. Smith as chief engineer, both recognized as able engineers, administrators, and forward-looking planners. The Minister, too, shared their mutual respect. The stage was set. The championship team had been put together!

Prior to this, the potential of his department had been under-utilized. The visionary, his feet firmly planted on the political ground, and with both the team and resources in place, moved swiftly ahead to put Ontario's highways in the forefront of the world's transportation networks. He did this, not by political whim or expediency. His approach was clearly a master plan to stimulate development, growth, and a solid future for Ontario's people and its resources, including tourism. All of this was to be scheduled on a logical scale of priorities, with an emphasis on immediate financial returns to underwrite the following stages.

First on the list was the transformation of a traditional, two-lane link, partly under construction, between Toronto and Hamilton into a great super-highway, sweeping from Toronto to Niagara Falls

The bridge at Ivy Lea spans the St. Lawrence.

and Buffalo. This road was to be built, using the most advanced technology which until then had never been implemented. Included were interchanges, overpasses, lane separation, and tasteful functional landscaping. In less than six years, the Queen Elizabeth Way was completed.

At the same time, efforts were directed to American border points to attract both business and tourism. New bridges, all award winners, were constructed at Sarnia (Blue Water), Gananoque (Ivy Lea), and Niagara Falls (Rainbow). Attendant road improvements, such as the four-lane scenic road along the St. Lawrence River, were initiated. Nor was the North neglected. The first paving in Northern Ontario took place, the road from North Bay to Timmins was brought near to completion. A highway across Ontario was completed, and the first piece of road from Hearst to Nipigon was built. The skill of the Ministry and its roadbuilders was eagerly sought in the frenzied construction of the Alaska Highway for the military concerns of the U.S. a few years later.

McQuesten's sense of history resulted in his ministry's reconstruction of Fort Henry and the Martello towers at Kingston. In his capacity as Chairman of the Niagara Parks Commission, he was responsible for similar works at Fort Erie and at

Fort Henry at Kingston — Parade Square and restored stone work.

Fort George in Niagara-on-the-Lake. One can only speculate how much more would have been created if the Federal Government had not been reluctant to participate. The grim realities of World War II gradually but firmly placed a clamp on all his more elaborate plans. The Burlington Skyway, planned in his era, did not become a reality for another quarter century. The concept of an encircling highway through the Red Creek Valley and around his City of Hamilton was a need he had envisioned and acted on in the past by land acquisition. Some 50 years after, local leaders still are struggling to implement his proposal. The long delay has been a costly impediment to the city's proper growth, prosperity, and aesthetic appeal.

Much more has been recorded of his Highways Ministry achievements, not the least of which is the creation of natural parks and campsites in scenic settings, particularly along the northern roads.

One of Ontario's most respected Conservative Premiers, Leslie Frost who had served in opposition to the Liberal government, was to remark later that "no Minister in the Liberal Cabinet was more beyond reproach or criticism than McQuesten in the highway portfolio." In Frost's position, perhaps this was the maximum accolade!

McQuesten at work in his office.

The Niagara Years

Chapter 5

The chairmanship of the Niagara Parks Commission was a mantle assumed by McQuesten along with his cabinet post. There is no evidence that any other person was considered for the position; McQuesten's reputation made certain of that. His activities in this position continued on a parallel path, for a decade, and were equal to those in his Highway Ministry. Commission affairs were given less than one day a week.

The Commission was a unique Crown Agency. It was the first expression of Canadian aspirations towards setting up national parks. Popular concern about the inroads of commercialism and the consequent spoiling of nature's great gift to America — Niagara Falls — had arisen, following the remarks of Lord Dufferin, Governor General of Canada. He had been inspired by earlier efforts made in the United States. One was a petition of March 2, 1880, signed by a galaxy of famous thinkers, among them Canadian and American political leaders, and such people as Thomas Carlyle, John Ruskin, Henry Longfellow, Ralph Waldo Emerson, Oliver Wendell Holmes, John Greenleaf Whittier, and others of equal stature. The total number amounted to nearly 700. Frederick Law Olmstead, America's great landscape architect, had before this endorsed corrective measures in a careful report with particular reference to the American side of the Falls. Premier Oliver Mowat, with his Liberal majority, quickly passed legislation in that same month of March 1880. The legislation clearly indicated that this was a matter for the Federal Government to pursue. Prime Minister Sir John A. Macdonald appears to have had other matters in mind, such as railways, and graciously declined to take any interest. As the Americans were moving more quickly to positive action, Mowat realized that

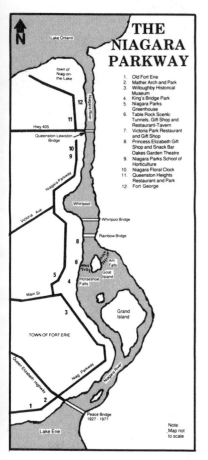

THE NIAGARA PARKWAY

1. Old Fort Erie
2. Mather Arch and Park
3. Willoughby Historical Museum
4. King's Bridge Park
5. Niagara Parks Greenhouse
6. Table Rock Scenic Tunnels, Gift Shop and Restaurant-Tavern
7. Victoria Park Restaurant and Gift Shop
8. Princess Elizabeth Gift Shop and Snack Bar Oakes Garden Theatre
9. Niagara Parks School of Horticulture
10. Niagara Floral Clock
11. Queenston Heights Restaurant and Park
12. Fort George

Note: Map not to scale

Ontario must act on its own. Finally, he introduced a measure entitled "An act for the preservation of the natural scenery about Niagara Falls", after a five-year wait for Federal Government action. On March 30, 1885, the Act was passed into legislation and is better known as the Niagara Falls Park Act.

Interestingly enough, Sir John A. Macdonald had a change of heart about national parks. Just six months later, in October 1885, he approved a motion to set aside a tract of land that was endowed with hot springs in Alberta. It eventually became known as Banff National Park—Canada's first National Park.

A commission was formed to study the matter and to report on the method of development and its probable cost. The first Chairman was Colonel Sir Casimir Gzowski, a lawyer, engineer, and businessman whose life and career have been detailed in this series, *The Canadians*. Through various steps, he and two other Commissioners acquired the most immediately connected land and set out to create a suitable public park. With the land, they acquired several attractive concessions that would produce money. Their job was to restore to some extent the natural scenery around the Falls of Niagara, to preserve the same from further deterioration, and to provide public facilities for observing the points of interest. Two indispensable conditions were added: that the Park should become self-supporting as soon as possible, but at the same time should be free to the public as far as possible. This was similar to the existing arrangement on the American side. The land-purchase cost and some initial operating costs were covered by the sale of bonds, backed by the Province of Ontario but to be repaid by the Commission. This was an excellent plan but it did not bear fruit in the first ten years. Only after the arrival of the hydro-electric age did the future brighten. Funds were gained from the sale of certain water rights belonging to the Niagara Parks Commission and a concession agreement to allow the operation of an electric trolley system. Both brought great difficulties. The park was continuously ravaged by hydro-electric power plant construction; and when the International Railway

Company expired it would receive from the
Commission a sum of money far in excess of all
revenues that it had created. It was actually
McQuesten who had to deal with the final
consequences of what others had set in motion.

However, with new revenues the Niagara Parks
Commission managed to attain the original
objective; to undertake some improvements and to
increase land holdings, largely through federal and
provincial land acquisition. In fact, during the
period 1924-1933, the Provincial Treasury siphoned
off some $3 500 000 from the Commission's profits.
This practice was discontinued under the new
Chairman!

With McQuesten's arrival, the stage was set for
the great steps forward to create the Niagara Parks
System, so well appreciated by today's public. There
could not have been a better leader. No public
official, before or since, has exhibited the vision
combined with the feelings of an artist and the skill
of the architect and engineer.

He truly created a century of beauty in a mere
five years (1934-1939). The intervention of a global
war cancelled his final five years of effort. No one
can know what else he would have accomplished.

The Niagara Parks System lies in a slender
strand along the entire west bank (the Canadian
Shore) of the Niagara River and is some 42 km (26
miles) in length. Under McQuesten, the slender
strand became like a necklace. "The Great Falls", as
the central gem, was part of a string of jewels —

*Canadian Falls in the area
of Table Rock in 1924.
Present visitors will never
see volume nor depth of
water equal to those shown
here. Diversion of water for
power generation in the
thirties and fifties has
reduced the flow.*

The front gates of Fort George as reconstructed in 1940. As in the original, timber was the main material.

THE MACKENZIE HOUSE

Recent modifications at the Mackenzie House show that the "original" pine board floors are supported by 20 cm thick re-inforced concrete sub-floors, added during the restoration. Only an earthquake will bring this house to a ruin!

Now maintained by the Niagara Parks Commission, this famous floral clock is a horticultural tourist landmark. It was originally built and operated by Ontario Hydro at the Queenston power plant.

selected tastefully for the various parkland settings along its length and held together by the immaculately groomed parkway.

In a north-to-south tour from Niagara-on-the-Lake, the tourist will find highlight after highlight along the way. At the start are Fort George and Navy Hall which have been restored from total ruin. McQuesten's tribute to the history of Upper Canada was accomplished with his personal touch for efficiency and economy. Government or Commission funds were spent as carefully as though they were his own. For example, using crown lands and the good will of his northern friends in Temagami, he acquired some 767 000 board feet of quality timber for around $22 000. An appraisal after delivery to Fort George valued the shipment at $77 000 (1987 — $4 000 000?).

South along the groomed parkway, a tourist would reach historic Queenston. Nearby, below the Escarpment, would be found the solidly rebuilt home and workshop of the rebel publisher William Lyon Mackenzie. A letter from his grandson, the Prime Minister of Canada, to McQuesten in 1935 expressed thanks for the tribute to his grandfather when he had been informed of the Commission's plans. Prime Minister Mackenzie King was already expressing a strong interest in ruins. He further expressed a hope that restoration would stabilize and protect the ruins. It seems that Mackenzie King was not beyond "looking a gift horse in the mouth", nor did he think of offering financial support or the gift of family heirlooms. He should have known McQuesten better. The house was completely rebuilt to last a few hundred years at least.

Above the Escarpment stands a completely renovated Queenston Heights Park, a favourite of area residents and tourists alike. It also houses perhaps the finest restaurant in the Parks System, solidly and tastefully built by T.B. in 1940.

Southward again on the parkway, the tourist will be drawn like a magnet to the School of Horticulture grounds. This world-renowned institution maintains some of the finest horticultural display gardens in North America, featuring a rose garden, herb garden, perennial gardens, and an

Brock's Monument and the Queenston Heights Restaurant as rebuilt in 1940.

arboretum that is said to contain a greater variety of trees and shrubs than any other collection in Canada. Within a year of McQuesten's arrival, he had installed K.M. Broman, his faithful lieutenant from the "North West Entrance" days, into the bureaucracy of the Commission to undertake greatly needed landscape improvements. Broman's major role was to found a School for Apprentice Gardeners. It was to be a residential school in an immaculate parklike setting, with an emphasis on practical training along with the needed theoretical studies.

T.B. McQuesten with the second graduating class of the N.P.C. School of Horticulture, instructors, staff, and several commissioners.
Front row: J. Ness, W. Love, R. Barnsley (author), T.B. McQuesten, D. Robertson, S. Lawlor, E. Hughes
Second row: G. Hamilton (Botanist), K.M. Broman, W. Schichlund, C.E. Kaumeyer (NPC), R. Lucas, J.M. Hardy
Back row: Dr. G. Snyder (NPC), J. Oaks (NPC), A. Haines (MPP)

The sod-breaking ceremony for the new Rainbow Bridge in 1940 — complete with a two-handled spade — shared by McQuesten and his American counterpart on the Niagara Falls Bridge Commission

Even McQuesten would never realize the full impact that this particular vision would have on Canadian parks and horticulture within the first 50 years. Nearly 400 graduates have completed the thorough three-year course and have made their contribution in the municipal parks system of nearly every Canadian city, as well as in the field of private enterprise and education. Very few of the graduates, perhaps less than ten per cent, have abandoned their horticultural trade or profession. Perhaps time will show this to be T.B. McQuesten's greatest continuing legacy, along with the Royal Botanical Gardens.

From the school southward, the parkway is noted for some 8 km (five miles) of protective parapet built of the finest silver-gray Queenston Dolomite Stone. For its erection, T.B. again had reached back to the talent he knew so well. From Hamilton, he brought a handful of Scottish stonemasons who accomplished the task in a few short years, when they were not building gates, buildings, flagstone walkways, and other garden features. McQuesten loved to build permanently with stone. Also from Hamilton, he brought Fred Flattman, an artist in wrought-iron work, to construct gates, grills, railings, and other decorative iron work.

Both the stone and the wrought iron can be seen in their full glory at the most impressive of his new gardens — The Oakes Garden Theatre and Rainbow Gardens adjacent to the Rainbow Bridge and Queen

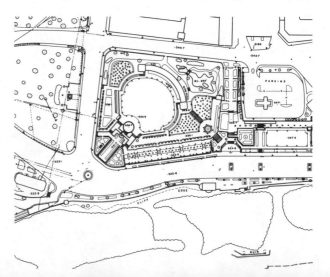

Site plan of Oakes Garden Theatre

*Opening ceremonies for the
Rainbow Bridge in 1941*

Victoria Park. For these intensive projects he again,
in loyalty and trust, secured the services of H.B.
Dunington-Grubb and his sculptress wife. The
garden was filled with classic features that included
parterres of clipped yew and box, espaliered trees
and shrubs, and a Japanese rock garden. All this
was surrounded by a magnificent pergola in stone
and timber. Its semi-circular shape provides at each
end a specific viewing point for each Falls, one the
American and one the Horseshoe Falls.

Carl Borgstrom also was not forgotten. He
received several smaller planning assignments and
the major responsibility for the Mather Park
development at Fort Erie. He worked on this project
with H.M. Carver and Earle Sheppard. At the
southerly terminus of the Parks System stands
another historic fort — Old Fort Erie — restored
from ruins to an outstanding memorial and prime
attraction.

The tourist, in this southward journey, has seen
much of McQuesten's work. To tell of much more, in

52

The completed Rainbow Bridge, bridge plaza, carillon tower, and Rainbow Gardens in 1955.

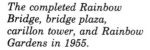

finer detail, would require a guidebook. What never will be mistaken is the overall expression of beauty and excellence in all the work he fathered. Such work likely never will be equalled and certainly never surpassed.

He left the Commission on August 10 of 1944, removed by the Conservative Government that had overturned his party in 1943. His political career was now over. In fact, he had less than three and a half years to live.

He returned to Hamilton to his law office and to the presidency of the Royal Botanical Gardens. His visits to Niagara for official reasons were now limited to the meetings of the Niagara Falls Bridge Commission.

In more than 100 years of Niagara Parks Commission history, no member of that Commission has approached T.B. McQuesten's insight into the original objectives of its founders. Nor have any matched his ability to create and blend beauty with making money. His successors have been caretakers, perhaps able, but lacking the dream of attaining the maximum potential of that great public asset — The Falls of Niagara.

The opening ceremony for Mather Park & Gate at Fort Erie. T.B. McQuesten is shown with younger friends.

The Royal Botanical Gardens

Chapter 6

No other project that McQuesten initiated had his involvement for such a long period of time. It covered the alderman's years preceding World War I and lasted to his final hours throughout 1947 and a few days into January of 1948.

The acquisition of parcels of lands in the McKittrick Survey (Westdale) during the late 1920s, less the area donated to McMaster University, can clearly be defined as the first steps towards the formation of a botanical garden. The presence of McMaster and its well-landscaped grounds added impetus to the idea. Two young students of that institution contributed to studies of the existing plant life. One was engaged by the Parks Board to make an inventory of the woody plants of the

Royal Botanical Gardens, the Laking Garden (formerly the Spring Garden). The High Level Bridge is at the upper left and Hamilton Mountain is in the background.

surrounding lands. Both, in part from these early opportunities, were stimulated to become expert botanists in their post-graduate studies in the United States and later in federal service and institutional careers. They were Dr. Harold A. Senn and Dr. James H. Soper. Another McMaster contribution was Dr. Norman Radforth, an expert in muskeg studies, who served as first director of the gardens.

In 1930, permission was granted on behalf of His Majesty King George the Fifth to use the word "Royal" in connection with the establishment of the Botanical Gardens at Hamilton. Concurrent with the "North West Entrance", additional reclaimed areas had been added to the growing accumulation of land. This included the now resplendent Rock Garden. Progress then slowed down, first because of the Depression and then World War II. By 1944, with his termination as N.P.C. Chairman, T.B.

Aerial view of the Spring Garden.

McQuesten returned in a more active role. He brought with him his faithful lieutenant, Matt Broman. He too had been a political victim at the N.P.C. He was simply struck from the payroll without formal notice or any thanks or consideration. Political appointments carried their hazards!

In 1941, McQuesten had passed an act respecting the Royal Botanical Gardens by setting up a Provincial Board, thus releasing the Hamilton Parks Board to some degree from the costly duty of funding the Gardens. There was a prospect of new development, with a potential broader base of support. With the war's closing days, a real start was made in creating many of the features that make up a meaningful botanic garden. Broman, in the role of planner-supervisor, constructed a Spring Garden, a children's garden, a plant nursery, propogating facilities, and the start of a large

Map of the Royal Botanical Gardens

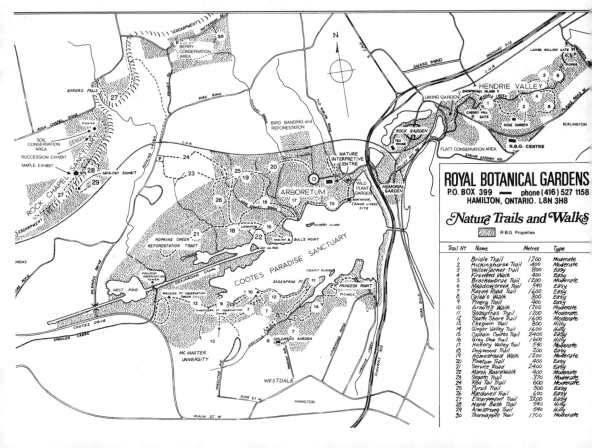

ROYAL BOTANICAL GARDENS
P.O. BOX 399 —— phone (416) 527 1158
HAMILTON, ONTARIO. L8N 3H8

Nature Trails and Walks

R.B.G. Properties

Trail Nº	Name	Metres	Type
1	Bridle Trail	1200	Moderate
2	Kickinghorse Trail	400	Moderate
3	Yellowjacket Trail	800	Easy
4	Fireweed Walk	400	Easy
5	Brackenbrae Trail	1200	Moderate
6	Meadowcreek Trail	540	Easy
7	Rayne Road Trail	1600	Easy
8	Caleb's Walk	800	Easy
9	Pinery Trail	600	Easy
10	Arnett's Walk	1200	Moderate
11	Sassafras Trail	1200	Moderate
12	South Shore Trail	1600	Moderate
13	Chegwin Trail	800	Hilly
14	Ginger Valley Trail	1600	Hilly
15	Captain Cootes Trail	2400	Easy
16	Grey Doe Trail	1600	Hilly
17	Hickory Valley Trail	590	Moderate
18	Dogwood Trail	200	Easy
19	Homestead Walk	1200	Moderate
20	Pinetum Trail	400	Easy
21	Service Road	2400	Easy
22	Marsh Boardwalk	400	Moderate
23	Segato Trail	370	Moderate
24	Red Tail Trail	600	Moderate
25	Pyrus Trail	500	Easy
26	Macdonell Trail	600	Easy
27	Escarpment Trail	3200	Easy
28	Maple Bush Trail	540	Hilly
29	Armstrong Trail	540	Hilly
30	Thornapple Trail	1700	Moderate

Some activities in the Children's Garden, 1962

arboretum. Staff were added, including Ray Halward as propagator and Leslie Laking, who later became curator and then director. The dream was now on its way to reality. Extensive natural areas were acquired and protected from development. Land area had been increased vastly, parts of it separated from each other by ravines, roads, and railways, but nevertheless a collective unit bringing nature directly into the heart of a growing, industrial city.

The growth and final form of the Royal Botanical Gardens was now assured, as was its future. With something approaching 1200 hectares (3000 acres) the Royal Botanical Gardens contributes handsomely to the cultural life of two regions and the Province of Ontario. It is, in fact, Ontario's only major botanical garden.

The Bitter Defeats

Chapter 7

In retrospect, the scope of the accomplishments dwarf all of T.B. McQuesten's defeats and lost causes. Politically, the 1923 failure to reach the Ontario Legislature provided a valuable lesson. His later victories in 1934 and 1937 made possible the full growth of his political career. Only the final loss in 1943 brought sorrow and anguish at the end of a magnificent career.

The battle of the railways in his council days may have dealt a sinister blow to Hamilton, his beloved city. To T.B. McQuesten, however, it became also a personal challenge. The T.H. and B. Railway Company expropriated the rear 15 m (50 feet) of Whitehern property for line improvements. The compensation for the property paid for the development of a beautiful town garden safely enclosed by a protective wall of limestone, and a useful addition, which included a study at the rear of his home.

A combination of the final political defeat, the weight and uncertainty of World War II, his declining health, and the last, dwindling opportunities for leadership left him in appearance a sorrowful and lonely figure, rather than the giant that he had been.

THE STORY OF THE BELLS

It is their story that erupted in the last months of his life that may have caused his loss of public acclaim far faster than his great contributions warranted.

It began with Hepburn's flouting Mackenzie King and the Federal Liberals in his acceptance of the Ontario leadership in 1933. The breach was never healed. The Ontario Liberals were an eternal thorn in the side of the Ottawa government on issue

Mitchell Hepburn in 1938 at Niagara Falls — as Ontario's premier

after issue related to the anemic war effort proposed by the King government, the Rowell-Sirois report, and the lack of support for many of McQuesten's developments, especially those with national and international significance. McQuesten's loyalty to his party and his leader could not escape King's wrath.

The Rainbow Bridge to the U.S.A. had been build without Ottawa's approval or support. Its cost had been born by American bondholders, American steel, and American engineers, under a formula that would have turned the bridge over to New York State and Ontario when the bonds were retired with the profits from the bridge tolls. With Canada at war and the U.S.A. at peace, it was a sound decision.

Included in the design was a large tower to hold a huge carillon of bells. On December 12, 1941, when ordering the bells, the Bridge Commission (created by Congress at Washington in 1937) approved an inscription on the large bell which included a verse and a credit to "Our Nations' Leaders — Winston Churchill and Franklin Roosevelt", which fairly represented the sentiments of the day in English Canada and the U.S. Because of wartime conditions, the British manufacturer did not deliver until after the war. After installation, furor broke out in Ottawa. McQuesten was to receive the brunt of the criticism and Ottawa (Mackenzie King and Lionel Chevrier) brought pressure on Ontario to remove McQuesten from his unpaid office on the Bridge Commission. Rightly or wrongly, he suffered the consequences and he never lived to hear the carillon played.

IN SUMMATION

The eulogies and tributes offered at the death of Thomas Baker McQuesten on January 13, 1948, were legion and superb in the thoughts they offered. The author believes that the greatest insights into his abilities and his character can be found in the two quotations that follow.

The first is not a eulogy, but the assessment of a keen contemporary reporter. The article "Hamilton's

Minister" (*Saturday Night* April 20, 1935) contains the observations of R.E. Knowles, Jr. and his advocacy of McQuesten as the most likely person to succeed [Hepburn] to the provincial Liberal leadership, *if* Mitchell Hepburn were to return to the federal field. He is quoted as follows:

"Many people will disagree. Other members of the Hepburn cabinet, they will point out, are much more in the public eye and therefore much more important than Mr. McQuesten. But aptitude for getting in the headline and a flair for startling statements are not the criteria of a cabinet minister's real importance. Executive ability, level-headedness, keen insight and the many desirable qualities implied by the word 'wisdom' are the factors that determine the standard of a man around the council board. None will deny that T.B. McQuesten possesses these qualities. Many will claim that he possesses them in greater measure than any of his cabinet colleagues. So, while other ministers may loom larger than he does (due to the distorted perspective created by the current scale of news values), Mr. McQuesten is none the less one of the outstanding members of the cabinet.

"When the cabinet is studying an especially ticklish problem, *more deference is paid to his views*, I am told, *than to those of any other minister. His opinions prevail and his suggestions are adopted*, it is said, *in nine cases out of ten* . . .

"His lips are firmly set, indicating inflexible resolution. He speaks slowly and deliberately — almost icily — as if carefully weighing each word. His presence suggests Efficiency with a capital E and a certain lack of the softer qualities such as sentimentality and excitability."

From the different perspective of a personal friend of 40 years and his minister for years, Dr. Beverley Ketchen quoted in eulogy:

"All his works praise him. You cannot look anywhere without seeing his monuments — the beauty spots which will be enjoyed by generations yet unborn and which will be admired by countless neighbours to the south of us.

"Mr. McQuesten had a rare and remarkable combination of gifts. Combined with his practical ability, and he had enough brains for half a dozen public men, he was a dreamer, a "healthy kind of visionary with a poetic passion for the beautiful.

"But his supreme interest was in the extension of God's Kingdom, an interest which made him 'more or less conspicuous among public men'.

"Tom loved beauty: beauty in literature, beauty in nature, beauty in music, in art and, above all, the supreme beauty, the beauty of Christ.

"Consequently, he enjoyed a wonderfully rich and abundant life, a very fitting kind of preface for the life he has now entered upon. He found God's work profitable for the life that is now his."

The Whitehern collection of family correspondence contains many tributes offered to the McQuesten family at the time of T.B.'s death. They

*Portrait of the Honourable
Thomas B. McQuesten
(1882-1948)*

were numerous and varied. They parallelled T.B.'s
life-long interests and were as diverse in source as
The Canadian Good Roads Association and the Guild
of Carilloneurs of North America. Others were
personal and political, equally fervent and sincere.

In the 40-50 years since the words of Knowles
and Ketchen, no evidence to diminish the man or
his works has been found. This is not surprising! It
is surprising, however, that recognition of his
contribution has been less than minimal.

The City of Hamilton accepted the family home,

Whitehern, on the death of the last McQuesten in 1968 and has created a fine museum in this prime example of 19th-century Ontario architecture. This is clearly a tribute to the three generations of McQuesten's that were its only occupants, not specifically to Thomas Baker McQuesten. The City also proposes to re-name the High Level Bridge in his honour on completion of repairs to the structure in 1988.

The Royal Botanical Gardens board has modestly acknowledged its founder. His portrait and office desk are displayed on the mezzanine of the headquarters building. The board also accepted a small memorial plaque, placed in the Rock Garden by T.B. McQuesten's dedicated secretary, Miss Jessie Yorston, who had served McQuesten both in his law practice and throughout his years as cabinet minister. The Province of Ontario, McQuesten's greatest beneficiary, has been more reluctant. It has, regrettably, never been in the nature of Ontario's political parties to acknowledge the accomplishments of their past political opponents in any meaningful way, no matter what their stature. This practice has been carried to extremes in the over 40-year span since McQuesten's death. In that interval, the Province has seen fit to honour the seventh* and eighth** chairmen of the Niagara Parks Commission, but continues to ignore the sixth — McQuesten. It is time to accept the true worth of a great contributor to Ontario's growth, and in a manner appropriate to his contribution.

In fact, the irony is the greatest in the case of the Niagara Parks Commission. It is this very agency that owes more to the McQuesten chairmanship than any other. In its 100-year history, more was accomplished from 1935 to 1939 than in the other 95 years. The very base of its fine reputation and growing revenues can be attributed to the developments and attractions conceived and executed by McQuesten.

*The Hon. Charles Daley 1944-67 — Charles Daley Park, 1962
**The Hon. James N. Allan, 1967-86 — James N. Allan
                              Burlington Skyway, 1985
                              — Pergola, School of
                              Horticulture, 1986

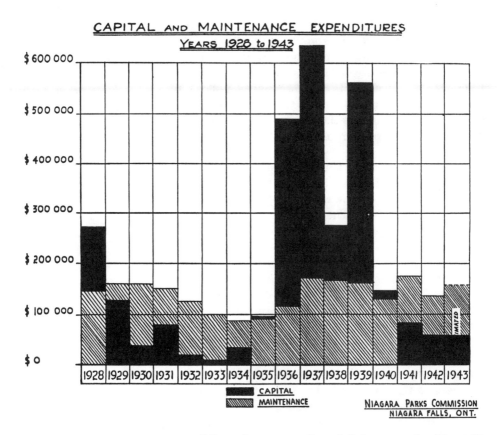

Others have questioned this anomaly. The editor of the Hamilton *Spectator* on April 20, 1971, can be quoted as follows:

JOHN SMITH, MOUNTAIN MLA, asked the Commission to name one of its new facilities, a park or monument, after Mr. McQuesten, pointing out that, during the man's provincial cabinet years, he established the Niagara Parks system, restored Forts George and Erie, and developed the beautiful border parkway.

Mr. Smith's thoroughly justified support of an oft-made proposal brought this prosaically bureaucratic reply from the general manager of Niagara Parks:

"It was the decision of the Commission that it did not wish to do anything further at this time. There are a number of past chairmen of the Commission who have not been recognized in this way.

"A plaque has been erected in the tower at the Niagara Falls Bridge Commission [a totally different jurisdiction!] and we plan to hang photographs of all the past Chairmen in the near future."

It can be recorded that the pictures were indeed hung in subsequent years! However, the chosen

SMOKE RINGS

The usual vices of life were frequently reported by the press in conjunction with many outside activities of the Hepburn Cabinet. At a point they ceased to be news! With the Honourable T.B. McQuesten it was a different matter. The evidence shows that he could be described as perilously close to being a teetotaler. Others claimed that he never smoked. On November 26, 1938, a Financial Post reporter had the assignment of covering a McQuesten speech (T.B. seldom made speeches) at the annual dinner of the Ontario Associated Boards of Trade and Chambers of Commerce. He found evidence to the contrary.

An extremely long introduction was accorded Thomas B. McQuesten, covering numerous events from 1882-1938 in great and lengthy detail. The reporter glossed over many of the highlights and concluded with the following paragraph:

> *"Mr. McQuesten is a bachelor and a continuing Presbyterian. He can blow excellent smoke rings! In fact the more Mr. Gray eulogized Ontario's Minister of Highways the faster the smoke rings pirouetted forth at the O.A.B. of T. and C. of C. function."*

No mention was made of the nature of T.B.'s speech!

---

location guaranteed that less than a handful of privileged visitors out of an estimated 15 000 000 annually would ever have the opportunity to view them. They decorate a small *private* room adjacent to the Commission Board Room!

Perhaps this quiet, giant of a man will remain Ontario's *Forgotten Builder* [*]— unless an ancient political bias and bureaucratic lethargy do not continue to obscure the man and his deeds.

---

[*] "The Forgotten Builder" — This was the title chosen by John Best, news editor of Channel 11 — CHCH TV for his documentary on T.B. McQuesten which was first aired on July 1, 1986. The author's path had converged with John's as they both researched the substantial and forgotten career of a most significant Canadian visionary and developer.

John Best's encouragement contributed greatly to the author's resolve to tell the McQuesten Story.

Further Reading

In *The Canadians* series: *Elizabeth Bagshaw, Adam Beck, Janet Carnochan, Casimir Gzowski, Tom Longboat, William Hamilton Merritt, Allan Napier MacNab*. Markham, Ontario: Fitzhenry & Whiteside Limited.

Campbell, Marjorie Freeman. *A Mountain and a City*. Toronto: McClelland & Stewart Ltd., 1966.

Forrester, James, Gary Birchall, and Douglas Gray. *Industrial Community*. Markham, Ontario: Fitzhenry & Whiteside Limited, 1982.

Katz, Michael B. *The People of Hamilton, Canada West*, Family and Class in a Mid-nineteenth Century City. Cambridge, Mass.: Harvard University Press, 1975.

McKenty, Neil. *Mitch Hepburn*. Toronto: McClelland & Stewart Ltd., 1967.

Siebel, George A. *Ontario's Niagara Parks — 100 Years*. Niagara Falls, Ontario: The Niagara Parks Commission, 1985.

Stamp, Robert M. *The World of Tomorrow*, A View of Canada in 1939. Markham, Ontario: Fitzhenry & Whiteside Limited, 1985.

Terpstra, Nicholas. *Local Politics and Local Planning*, A Case Study of Hamilton, Ontario. In *Urban History Review* XIV No. 2, October 1985.

Way, Ronald L. *Ontario's Niagara Parks, A History*. Revised Edition. Niagara Falls, Ontario: The Niagara Parks Commission, 1960.

Acknowledgements and Credits

John Best   CHCH TV Eleven, Hamilton, Ontario
Lou Cahill   Ontario Editorial Bureau, St. Catharines, Ontario
Ania Latoszek   Curator of Whitehern, Department of Culture and Recreation, Hamilton, Ontario
To all of the above, for their generous gift of time, advice, and shared enthusiasm, the author is most grateful.

Photo Credits

Roland Barnsley, 13, 24, 32
Wayne Farrar, cover photo of Niagara Falls
Hamilton Public Library, 6, 23, 27, 30, 31, 33
Hamilton *Spectator*, 36
Niagara Parks Commission, 4, 25, 47, 48, 49, 50 (bottom), 52, 62
Public Archives Canada, (C24696) 40, (C19529) 58
Royal Botanical Gardens, 5, 29, 53, 54, 55, 56
St. Lawrence Parks Commission, 43
Toronto Historical Board, 11
"Whitehern", Department of Culture and Recreation, Corporation of the City of Hamilton, cover portrait, 1, 7, 9, 10, 14, 15, 16, 17, 19, 20, 21, 42, 44, 50 (top), 51, 60

Index